GODS AND GODDESSES
OF
ANCIENT ROME

LEON ASHWORTH

SMART APPLE MEDIA

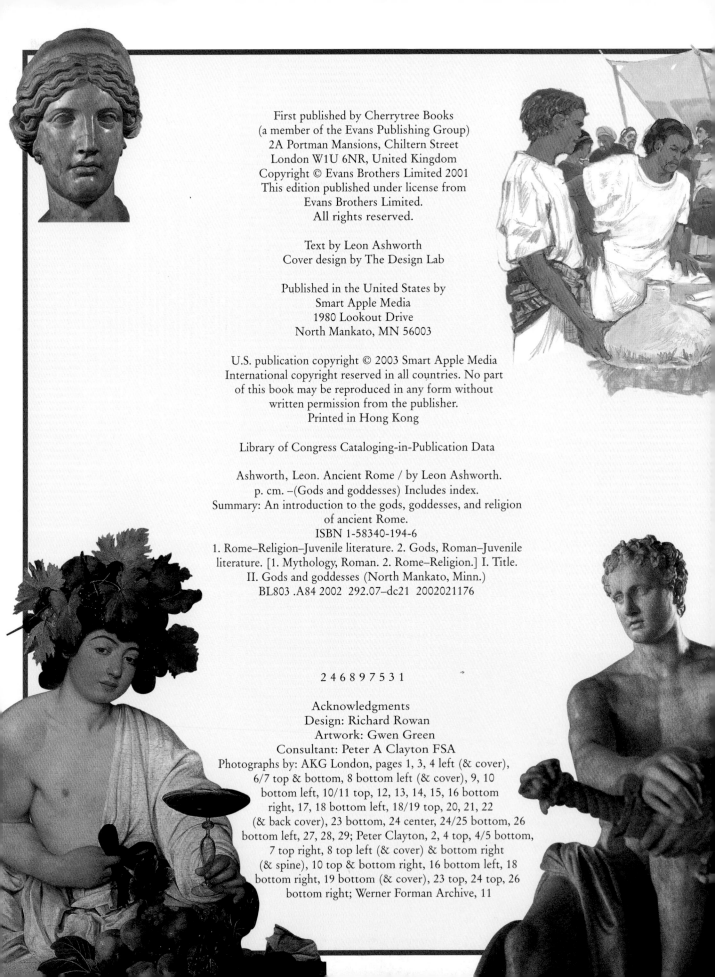

First published by Cherrytree Books
(a member of the Evans Publishing Group)
2A Portman Mansions, Chiltern Street
London W1U 6NR, United Kingdom
Copyright © Evans Brothers Limited 2001
This edition published under license from
Evans Brothers Limited.

Text by Leon Ashworth
Cover design by The Design Lab

Published in the United States by
Smart Apple Media
1980 Lookout Drive
North Mankato, MN 56003

Printed in Hong Kong

Library of Congress Cataloging-in-Publication Data

Ashworth, Leon. Ancient Rome / by Leon Ashworth.
p. cm. –(Gods and goddesses) Includes index.
Summary: An introduction to the gods, goddesses, and religion
of ancient Rome.
ISBN 1-58340-194-6
1. Rome–Religion–Juvenile literature. 2. Gods, Roman–Juvenile
literature. [1. Mythology, Roman. 2. Rome–Religion.] I. Title.
II. Gods and goddesses (North Mankato, Minn.)
BL803 .A84 2002 292.07–dc21 2002021176

2 4 6 8 9 7 5 3 1

Acknowledgments
Design: Richard Rowan
Artwork: Gwen Green
Consultant: Peter A Clayton FSA
Photographs by: AKG London, pages 1, 3, 4 left (& cover),
6/7 top & bottom, 8 bottom left (& cover), 9, 10
bottom left, 10/11 top, 12, 13, 14, 15, 16 bottom
right, 17, 18 bottom left, 18/19 top, 20, 21, 22
(& back cover), 23 bottom, 24 center, 24/25 bottom, 26
bottom left, 27, 28, 29; Peter Clayton, 2, 4 top, 4/5 bottom,
7 top right, 8 top left (& cover) & bottom right
(& spine), 10 top & bottom right, 16 bottom left, 18
bottom right, 19 bottom (& cover), 23 top, 24 top, 26
bottom right; Werner Forman Archive, 11

CONTENTS

ANCIENT ROME

THE STORY of Rome and its gods began more than 2,000 years ago, in 753 B.C., when the city of Rome is said to have been founded. The city grew up around seven hills alongside the river Tiber in central Italy (see map page 31). Being on a river, the place was good for farming and for trade. The people became rich and powerful, taking over neighboring cities and governing them well. With their great army, the Romans went on to conquer the rest of Italy and, in time, most of Europe and beyond.

ADOPTED GODS

In ancient times, only the Jews worshipped a single god. Other ancient peoples, including the Romans, worshipped many gods. They believed that the gods controlled every part of their lives. If one needed help, it was important to know the right god to ask for it. The gods did not always behave well. They carried on in what most people today would regard as a quite ungodly way.

As the Romans conquered new lands and peoples, they gathered new gods and

ROMULUS AND REMUS

According to legend, Romulus and Remus were twin sons of the god Mars. Their mother's wicked uncle set the babies adrift on the river Tiber in a basket. They were saved from death by a she-wolf who looked after them as her own. The boys were later found by a herdsman who brought them up. As young men they founded the city of Rome. But the two quarreled, and Romulus killed Remus. The surviving twin gave his name to the city. The coin above shows the she-wolf suckling the twins.

◀ **The Romans made statues of their gods and goddesses, many of which have survived unharmed. Unfortunately, this statue of the goddess Minerva has lost its arm.**

FAMILY OF THE ROMAN GODS

SATURN
father of the gods

NEPTUNE
god of the sea

VESTA
goddess of fire and the hearth

JUPITER
supreme god and god of the sky

=

JUNO
mother goddess

CERES
goddess of crops

PLUTO
god of the underworld

MERCURY
winged messenger of the gods

MINERVA
goddess of wisdom

BACCHUS
god of wine

APOLLO
god of the sun

DIANA
goddess of the moon

VULCAN
god of fire and forge

=

VENUS
goddess of love

MARS
god of war

CUPID
god of love

▲ The Roman gods were descended from Saturn. There were 12 great gods— Jupiter, Juno, Vesta, Minerva, Ceres, Diana, Venus, Mars, Mercury, Neptune, Vulcan, and Apollo. The family tree shows the relationships between the gods.

= MARRIAGE

◄ Rome had many temples. This is the temple of Saturn. Little of the building now remains, but Saturn lives on in the name for Saturday.

goddesses. They let conquered people worship their own gods, so long as they also worshipped Roman gods. Many of these gods were simply Greek gods with a different name (see page 31). People in different places told different stories about the gods, but that did not matter.

Eventually, led by the emperor Constantine, the Romans gave up their gods and came to believe in a single god. They adopted the Christian religion.

ROMAN RELIGION

RELIGION WAS part of everyday life. People had shrines in their homes and visited temples. The rulers of Rome made no decisions without consulting priests. Farmers planted crops only when the gods wished them to, and army commanders relied on the gods for aid in battle.

Roman religion was about the family first, and then about the state—the "family of Rome." In most homes, the family said prayers every day, and their main meal was itself a religious ceremony.

PRIESTS AND AUGURS

Festivals and religious ceremonies were run by priests. They kept traditions, followed the rules, and recorded important events. Priests were helped by soothsayers, or augurs. These wise men could tell what the gods wanted. They "read" signs in the sky, such as thunderstorms, clouds, lightning, and the flights of birds. They examined the entrails (insides) of sacrificed

RITUAL SACRIFICE

Rituals were held outside the temple on a marble altar. People might bring a chicken, a sheep, or even a bull to be sacrificed. Priests and their helpers would hang garlands of flowers around the animal's

VISITING THE TEMPLE

Roman temples usually housed a large statue of the god, lit by flickering oil lamps. Individuals would stand before the statue to make their requests for help and place an offering of money or a small statue on the ground. Some might leave a curse against an enemy. There were no religious services inside the temple for people to attend.

neck and anoint it with oils. Then they would cut its throat and throw its body onto a brazier to cook while the augurs checked the innards. In this carving, a Roman emperor prepares to sacrifice a bull.

animals. From these omens, they proclaimed what the gods approved or disapproved.

FESTIVALS

Most festivals were seasonal. There was a sowing festival in spring and a harvest festival in the autumn. The longest festival was the seven-day Saturnalia in December. Saturn was one of the old gods of Italy, who ruled in the "golden age" before Rome was founded. During his festival, schools and law courts closed, business stopped, and everyone feasted, often remaining at the table all day. Masters served their slaves, who in memory of the golden age could do and say what they liked. This merry-making tradition is still carried on at Christmas.

▼ The Romans loved to dance at their summer festivals. This picture shows the god Apollo dancing with the Nine Muses (see page 30). Their names are written in Greek.

▲ A small bronze statue of a priest found in northern England, from the time when the Romans conquered Britain.

GODS OF THE CITY

ROME WAS a great city with many fine buildings and rich citizens. The citizens kept their peace with the gods. So long as the gods were on their side, their city would be safe.

VESTA AND THE SACRED FLAME

The goddess Vesta guaranteed the survival of the city, and every family had a shrine to her. Vesta was the daughter of Saturn and the goddess of fire. In her temple, a perpetual flame burned. The flame symbolized Roman belief that their city would last forever. The sacred flame was renewed every year on the first day of March, Rome's New Year.

JANUS, THE GOD WITH TWO FACES

Janus was the god of gateways. His two faces enabled him to look both ways—in and out—and watch over the inside and outside of houses. Statues of Janus show him with a key (for opening the gates) and a stick (to drive intruders away). Janus knew the past and future and was a great warrior.

VESTAL VIRGINS

Vesta's temple and flame were looked after by priestesses called Vestal Virgins, who were like nuns. There were six of them, chosen by lot from noble families and instructed from childhood in their duties. The girls were sacred and not

JANUS SAVES ROME

During an attack on Rome by a hostile tribe called the Sabines, a Roman woman was bribed with jewels to show the enemy the path to the citadel. Janus saw the danger and caused a jet of boiling water to spring up. The steaming fountain halted the Sabines in their tracks. The god's temple was built on the spot. This coin shows the two-faced head of Janus.

◄ The temple of Vesta was one of the most important in Rome. In it burned an eternal flame, tended by young women called Vestal Virgins.

▲ A bust of Octavian, who ruled so wisely as emperor that the people gave him the title Augustus and proclaimed him a living god. The month of August is named after him.

allowed to mix with boys or to marry. The innermost sanctuary of Vesta's temple was opened once a year to mothers, who visited it barefoot with gifts of food.

His temple gates were open only in time of war—which was most of the time—until the emperors Augustus and Nero brought a few periods of peace to the empire.

The Romans gave Janus credit for starting most things. He was the god of daybreak, and the month of January (the opening of the year) is named after him. He was also the god of departure and return, and Romans relied on him as they navigated their ships in and out of harbors.

▲ The remains of the Forum, the main meeting place in ancient Rome. Today, it is a ruin (above), but in Roman times, it was full of activity and the bustle of daily life (below).

GODS OF THE HOME

THE ROMANS believed that certain gods looked after their homes and possessions. Every family hearth had a shrine with statues of Vesta and lesser household gods called Lares and Penates. Vesta presided over the preparation and eating of meals.

Every day, the family made offerings to their gods: portions of the family meal, dishes of special cakes, honey, wine, and incense. The Penates made sure the family had enough food and drink. They protected the entire household, but took particular care of the storeroom. When a family moved, so did the spirits who watched over the household. It was easy to carry their small statues to the new home.

GUARDIANS AND GUIDES

Every boy and girl had a personal spirit to watch over them and shape their character and personality. Boys had a Genius, girls had a Juno. These spirits had various helpers—one made the baby cry for the first time, another taught it to eat and drink, two more taught it to walk, and so on.

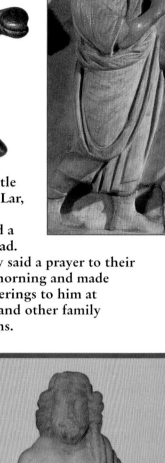

▲ This little statue is a Lar, holding a platter and a loaf of bread. The family said a prayer to their Lar each morning and made special offerings to him at weddings and other family celebrations.

◄ Babies were carefully watched over, with a separate god to oversee every aspect of an infant's life.

▲ All the children of the family were taught about the gods and learned to respect them. This boy is being taught rhetoric—the art of public speaking—by his tutor.

MORNINGS WITH THE GODS

Every morning, Romans made offerings to their household gods, as Hindu families do today. After breakfast, the son of this family gets ready to walk to school with his slave. His sister will stay at home with her mother and learn the skills of running a large household.

GODS WHO CARED

Aesculapius God of medicine (left, with Hygeia)
Bonus Eventus God who brought success in enterprises and made things turn out for the best
Deverra Spirit of the broom (for sweeping clean)
Fortuna Goddess of chance, who could tell the future
Hygeia Goddess of health; the daughter (sometimes wife) of Aesculapius
Hymen God of marriage
Orbona Goddess who looked after orphans
Pilumnus and Picumnus Twin gods who looked after newborn babies
Terminus God who watched over property
Viriplace God who soothed quarrels between husbands and wives

▼ This family altar from Pompeii shows two household gods dancing on either side of the master of the house. The snake below symbolizes the Genius of the house.

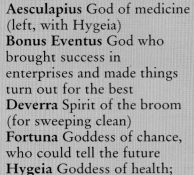

JUPITER AND JUNO

JUPITER WAS ruler of the universe. This great sky god did exactly as he pleased. He created storms and lightning, and hurled thunderbolts in anger. People had every reason to fear him and hold him in awe.

Jupiter was also a warrior god, who inspired Rome's army. After winning battles, generals offered Jupiter a gold crown of victory. Each year, the Romans played games in his honor, including running and chariot races.

JUNO'S SACRED GEESE

Sacred geese kept at Juno's temple on the Capitol (the center of Rome) once saved Rome from its enemies. When invading Gauls tried to climb the walls of the citadel, the geese's cackling warned Rome's defenders in time to drive off the attack.

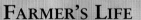

FARMER'S LIFE

Most Romans were farmers. They relied on the soil and the weather, so they took pains never to anger Jupiter since he controlled the sun, wind, rain, and everything that affected their lives. The Romans grew corn for making bread, olives for making oil, and grapes for making wine. Slaves worked

▲ A bust of Juno from Rome. The month of June is named after her. Juno was usually shown with her peacock, Argus, by her side.

◀ Jupiter, the chief Roman god, stands at his altar. The eagle at his feet represents his power.

the fields for their master landowners. Sudden rainstorms caused by Jupiter's wrath could ruin the harvest.

JUNO, SISTER AND WIFE

Juno was Jupiter's sister as well as his wife. She was a mother goddess, who looked after women, marriage, and childbirth. As the ideal woman, she became the symbol of the perfect Roman wife and mother. But Juno's husband was not perfect, and the goddess had many rivals for his affections. In fits of jealous rage, Juno often took revenge on them. Jupiter and Juno, together with Jupiter's favorite daughter, Minerva (see page 22), were among Rome's most important gods.

JUPITER'S SACRED COW

Jupiter used all kinds of tricks to stop his wife from finding out about his adventures. To avoid his wife attacking Io, a nymph (see page 23) with whom he had fallen in love, Jupiter turned the girl into a beautiful white cow. This 17th-century painting shows Jupiter presenting the transformed nymph to his wife. The largest moon of the planet Jupiter is named after Io.

13

NEPTUNE, GOD OF THE SEA

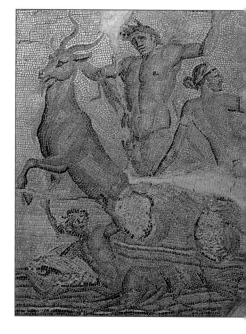

THE GOD Neptune shared with his brothers the wealth of their father, Saturn. Jupiter won the earth, Pluto the underworld, and Neptune the sea. Neptune, in his palace beneath the waves, had total power over the sea and those who sailed on it. With his weapon, the trident, he could raise storms or calm the raging waves. When angry, he could cause shipwrecks, split rocks, and create earthquakes.

The Romans depended on the sea for fishing and trading, and for transporting troops. Sea travel was dangerous. Sailors, traders, and fishermen prayed to Neptune to keep them safe, and visited his shrine to give thanks when they returned home safely.

In the hot Italian summer, the Romans celebrated the festival of Neptune, who was also the

AENEAS AND THE STORM

The poet Virgil told this story about Aeneas, a hero who had angered the goddess Juno. When Aeneas set sail with his fleet, Juno rushed to the wind god Aeolus in his underwater cave. She begged him for a storm to kill Aeneas. In return, she offered him a beautiful sea nymph. Aeolus at once set free his four winds (below). They churned up the waves and shattered the ships, tossing masts, beams, and sailors overboard like sticks of wood. Aeneas prayed, but the gods seemed deaf. Then Neptune in his ocean depths noticed wreckage and bodies sinking to the sea bed. He recognized the wicked work of Juno. Furious, he called the winds to cease. Then, riding over the waters, he calmed them so that Aeneas could sail on with what was left of his fleet.

▲ Tritons, nereids (sea nymphs), and a sea-antelope are pictured on this Roman mosaic. Tritons were descendants of Neptune's son. The Romans believed these mermen caused shipwrecks and other mishaps at sea.

▲ A merman (half-man, half-fish) is pictured on this ancient pot. Neptune's son Triton was a merman.

AT NEPTUNE'S MERCY

Neptune's symbol of power was a trident, a three-pronged spear used by Roman fishermen. His goodwill was vital to them. In addition to small fishing boats, the Romans had wide sailing ships for carrying goods, and ships called galleys for transporting troops or fighting battles. Sea travel was rarely undertaken during winter for fear of Neptune's storms.

god of freshwater rivers, lakes, and streams. Farmers needed the god's help to keep water flowing for their ripening crops.

NEPTUNE'S FAMILY

Neptune and his wife, the sea nymph Amphitrite, had a son called Triton, who was half-man, half-fish. He acted as a messenger and herald for his father, blowing on a conch shell to stir up the waters or calm them. When a human horn player called Misenus challenged his skill, Triton caused him to drown.

◀ Neptune rode the seas in a horse-drawn chariot, attended by dolphins. He was god of horses as well as the sea, and father of the famous winged horse, Pegasus.

PLUTO AND THE UNDERWORLD

THE ROMANS believed that when they died they would go to the underworld, which was deep in the center of the earth. It was reached through openings such as caves or deep lakes. King of the underworld was Pluto, brother of Jupiter. He had a thick beard and held a black scepter and fork. People found him gloomy, but not frightening. He was linked to cypress trees, which are a symbol of grief and are often grown in Italian graveyards.

ORPHEUS AND EURYDICE

The Romans loved this old Greek story. Orpheus was a miraculous musician. He sang and played the lyre so sweetly that animals followed him, and rivers became still to listen. When his wife Eurydice died, Orpheus followed her soul to the underworld. His music so charmed Pluto and Proserpina that they agreed to let Eurydice return to life and daylight, on condition that Orpheus did not look back on the upward journey. The pair set off, but Orpheus could not resist a backward glance. As he did so, Eurydice vanished and was lost to him forever.

CERES AND PROSERPINA

Pluto was so ugly that he could find no girl willing to be his wife. So he captured Proserpina, the beautiful daughter of Ceres, the goddess of corn

▼ **This Roman floor mosaic shows Orpheus charming the beasts with his music.**

ROMAN FUNERALS

When a Roman citizen died, his wife would let her hair hang loose as a sign of grief. Slaves would wait for the man's will to be read, for it was the custom for some slaves to be freed when their master died. At the funeral, these ex-slaves carried his body on an

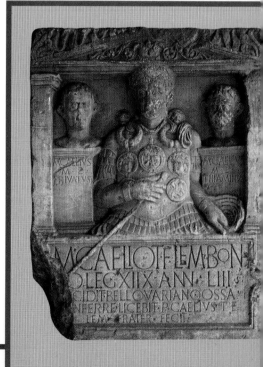

open bier. Priests led the funeral procession and prayers. Musicians played mournful music, and women wailed. A member of the family made a speech in praise of the man. Then he was buried in a tomb outside the town. The picture in the panel (below left) shows the tombstone of a centurion and two freed slaves.

PEOPLE AND PLACES OF THE DEAD

Genii Protective spirits who escorted the dead on their journey through the afterlife
Hell The place where wicked people are punished after they die
Lake Avernus near Pozzuoli had links to the underworld; its wooded hills were pitted with caverns through which (so it was believed) the dead could be summoned
Lemures Mischievous ghosts who came back from the dead to torment the living
Orcus God of death (often confused with Pluto) who carried off people by force

and plenty, and carried her off to his underground kingdom to be his queen.

Ceres looked everywhere for her lost daughter. Finally she gave up hope of finding her on earth and lit a torch to light her way into the darkness of the underworld. There she pleaded with Pluto and threatened to destroy the world by famine. But Pluto would not give up his bride. So Ceres carried out her threat. She caused a drought so severe that farm crops everywhere withered in the sun. Nothing would grow.

To prevent disaster Jupiter had to act. He ruled that Proserpina should stay above ground with Ceres for six months, and return to live with Pluto for the other six. For the Romans, this myth explained the changing of the seasons, from the bright days of summer to the gloom of winter.

▲ An ancient tomb painting showing a dead soul being escorted to the underworld by genii.

MARS AND VULCAN

F IGHTING WAS a way of life for the Romans. They marched across Europe, defeating hostile tribes and making them part of their empire. Roman generals and their troops trusted in the gods to bring them victory, and the gods did so almost unfailingly.

MARS AND VENUS

Mars showed the gentler side to his nature when he fell in love with Venus, the goddess of love and beauty. She alone was able to subdue his warlike temper. Cupid was their son. But like some of the other gods, Mars found it difficult to remain faithful. He fell in love with at least two Vestal Virgins, persuading them to forget their vows. One of them, Rhea Silvia, gave birth to his two sons—Romulus and Remus (see page 4). This wall painting (below) from Pompeii shows Mars and Venus at home with their son Cupid.

MARS, GOD OF WAR

Mars was the son of Juno and father of Romulus and Remus. After Jupiter, he was the Romans' most important god. The first month of the old Roman year was March. It marked the beginning of spring and was dedicated to Mars because in the old days, when the Romans were simple farmers, he was their god of fertility and farming. As the Romans moved from farming to empire-building, they made

▲ Roman soldiers looked to Mars to bring them victory in war.

▼ A bronze statue of the fiery god Vulcan. His anger was made worse by his wife Venus, who was often unfaithful to him.

THE ROMAN ARMY

Roman soldiers were well armed and well trained. When the army was on the move, the foot soldiers marched 18 miles (30 km) or more in a day, carrying all their gear and rations. Discipline could be harsh, but there were honors and rewards. Retired soldiers were often given land to farm. The Romans honored Mars with competitions that included warlike sports and horse races.

their favorite Mars into their god of war, which was now their main concern.

VULCAN, THE FIERY BLACKSMITH

Vulcan was the god of fire, metalworking, and craftsmanship. He was the blacksmith of the gods, hammering armor and weapons, some of them magical. He made Jupiter's thunderbolts and could start and control the spread of fire. Vulcan's forge was under Mount Etna, the volcano on the island of Sicily.

To punish Venus, goddess of love, for her pride, Jupiter made her marry the fiery Vulcan, who was lame and ugly. On Vulcan's chief festival day, the Romans threw offerings of fish into a sacred fire, perhaps because water creatures were normally beyond the god's reach.

◀ This statue shows Mars as strong and powerful. Tuesday was his day, still recalled in the French name of *Mardi*.

19

APOLLO AND DIANA

LIKE THE people of most early civilizations, the Romans believed that the sun and the moon were gods. People also believed that the stars influenced their lives. It was the job of Roman astrologers to tell the future from the movements of the stars.

APOLLO, THE SUN GOD

Apollo was one of Jupiter's many children. A famous Greek story told how, as a four-day-old baby, Apollo fought and killed the serpent-monster Python, which had tried to kill his mother, Leto.

Apollo left the realm of the gods and for many years roamed the world, slaying giants with his arrows and even challenging the mighty Hercules (see page 26). Jupiter had to make peace between the two warriors.

Perhaps to keep his son out of further trouble, Jupiter gave him the task of spreading light across

▲ This is a Roman copy of a Greek head of Apollo. The Romans thought Apollo was the ideal young man.

▶ This sculpture shows Diana the huntress fastening her robe.

▼ Apollo stands with the centaur Chiron and the Greek doctor Hippocrates in this wall painting from Pompeii.

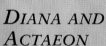

DIANA AND ACTAEON

Diana's beauty attracted hopeful lovers, but she would have none of them. A famous story told how she was pursued by the hunter Actaeon. In her anger, the goddess turned him into a stag, which was then pursued and killed by Actaeon's own hounds. This detail from a mosaic floor shows Diana hunting, riding on a stag.

FEAST OF DIANA

Diana was the protector of the lower classes. Her festival on August 13 was a holiday for Roman slaves, who held merry celebrations in her honor. They gathered near the steps of her temple to drink and dance into the night.

the world. In a chariot made by Vulcan, Apollo drove the sun across the sky each day from dawn to dusk.

Apollo enjoyed eternal youth and had many love affairs. He chased Daphne, a maiden from Thessaly, until she turned into a laurel bush in order to escape him. To attract the nymph Driope, the god took the form of a tortoise.

As well as being the god of light, Apollo was also the god of medicine, archery, poetry, arts, and music. He played a lyre, a stringed instrument invented by his little brother Mercury. He was also a shepherd-god, protecting flocks.

DIANA, GODDESS OF THE MOON

Diana was Apollo's twin sister and goddess of the moon. She flew across the heavens in a chariot drawn by a flock of doves. On earth, Diana was the goddess of woods and the hunt. She was often shown with a bow and quiver, and accompanied by a hound or a deer.

Diana was so beautiful that many gods and mortals fell in love with her, but she rejected them all. Even so, women who wanted to have babies said special prayers to her.

MERCURY AND MINERVA

T HE ROMANS brought law and order—and peace—to the world. This encouraged trade, for traders could move their goods around without fear of robbers or pirates. The god of trade was Mercury, but he was also the god of thieves.

MERCURY, MESSENGER OF THE GODS

Mercury was another of Jupiter's sons. He was the winged messenger of the gods, a small, clever, cunning individual who was a jack-of-all-trades. He was the god not just of traders and thieves, but also of gamblers, orators, travelers, merchants, and industry. He was shown holding a purse full of money and had a salesperson's easy way with words. He was always ready to help and always on the move.

One of Mercury's roles was to guide adventurers and travelers. Some say he led the souls of the dead to the underworld. His magic powers and unearthly

▲ This bronze bust of Minerva shows her wearing her helmet. Above all the other gods, she was credited with tactical skill in warfare.

MERCURY'S WINNING WAYS

When he was just one day old, Mercury showed his cleverness by making a lyre for his brother Apollo. He then displayed his criminal side by stealing Apollo's oxen. Apollo took him to Jupiter for a scolding, but little Mercury got off lightly. He played the lyre so beautifully that Jupiter's anger turned to pleasure at his son's brilliance. He gave Mercury a winged cap, winged shoes, and the job of gods' messenger.

MERCHANTS

Goods brought in from the countryside or made in workshops were sold in Rome's shops and markets. Traders used scales to weigh goods, and standards were strictly enforced. Weights and measures, and the values of coins, were the same throughout the empire. People carried their money in small leather pouches, just like Mercury.

speed made him a useful friend. The French keep his name in *Mercredi* (Wednesday).

MINERVA, GODDESS OF WISDOM

Minerva was one of the greatest goddesses. She was the goddess of wisdom and good advice, the art of warfare, science, and all arts and skills, especially weaving and spinning. She was the patron of cobblers, carpenters, artists, poets, doctors, and schools. People believed that anything she promised would come about. Her shrine was a meeting place for craftsmen, poets, and actors.

Minerva was often shown wearing a helmet and holding a spear and a magic shield. Sometimes she held a distaff (used for spinning), and sometimes the twig of an olive tree. Her animals, the owl and the cock, were always near her.

▲ This small statue of Mercury shows him carrying his purse and his caduceus. This rod with two snakes coiled about it symbolized his importance as a sacred messenger.

MERCURY AND ARGUS

Mercury was always ready to lend a hand with his father's love affairs. Jupiter loved Io and had turned the beautiful girl into a cow in order to deceive his wife. He gave the beast to Juno, but she was not fooled and kept the cow well guarded by a 100-eyed man named Argus. Mercury slew Argus, whose eyes were transferred by Juno to the tail of the peacock. In his version of the legend, the painter Rubens shows Mercury lulling Argus to sleep with his flute so that he can cut off his head and steal the cow away.

VENUS AND CUPID

ROMANTIC LOVE played little official part in the lives of most Romans. Juno presided over marriage. In patrician (upper class) families, daughters might be only 12 when they married and might take no part in choosing their husband. Plebeians (working-class people) had more freedom, but little time for romance, while slaves were too busy working. But love finds a way, and in Rome its way was led by Venus and her son Cupid.

CUPID AND PSYCHE

Psyche was a princess who was so beautiful that Venus was mad with jealousy. In her fury, she told Cupid to make Psyche fall in love with the ugliest man in the world. Unfortunately, when Cupid saw Psyche, he scratched himself with one of his own arrows, and promptly fell in love with her himself. To avoid upsetting his mother, he visited Psyche only at night and told her that she must never see him in the light. But Psyche disobeyed him and lit a lamp to snatch a glimpse of him. At once, he deserted her, leaving her to wander the world trying to find him. Spiteful Venus did her best to make Psyche's plight more miserable. But in the end, soft-hearted Jupiter took pity on the poor girl. He granted her immortality, and she and Cupid were reunited. This 15th-century picture shows episodes from the story.

VENUS, GODDESS OF LOVE AND BEAUTY

Venus was at first the goddess of gardens. She was especially important to the Romans, who believed she was the mother of the whole

▶ This little statue of Venus shows her crowned and carrying the apple she won as the prize in the beauty contest judged by the hero Paris.

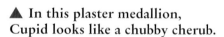

▲ In this plaster medallion, Cupid looks like a chubby cherub.

human race. Venus was famous for her beauty. In a beauty contest judged by Paris, prince of Troy, she defeated both Juno and Minerva to win the prize. Venus is usually shown as a young, smiling girl. The goddess was the wife of Vulcan, but Mars probably was the father of her son, although in some stories Jupiter or Mercury is his father.

CUPID, GOD OF LOVE

Cupid was a playful lad with a bow and arrows. His arrows were full of passion, and whoever was struck by them fell in love. In statues, the Romans made him a naked, winged boy (rather like a cherub).

The little love-god was also blindfolded, to show that "love is blind" and that Cupid shot his love-darts without knowing whom they might hit. The Romans carved pictures of him (often asleep or drunk) on tombstones, to represent the pleasant sleep of death.

A WEDDING

On her wedding day, a Roman bride was led to her new home by torchbearers and musicians. Three friends of the bridegroom would carry her over the threshold so that her feet would not touch the ground.

CERES AND COUNTRY GODS

THE ROMANS were, first of all, farmers and shepherds. They believed in a great many spirits of nature, some wild and mischievous, others generous and helpful. Even when they ruled a vast empire and many people lived in cities, they still felt attached to the simple, country life. Many patricians had country estates, and retired soldiers were rewarded with country properties.

GOD OF FLOCKS

Faunus was half-goat and half-man, a wild god of the hills and the flocks of animals that roamed them. Like the shepherds who tended their flocks on the hillsides, Faunus played panpipes, an instrument named after the Greek god Pan. The pipes were said to have been invented by the nymph Syrinx, who escaped the god's unwanted attentions only by turning herself into a clump of reeds.

FAUNUS AND HERCULES

Faunus was always eager to try his luck with girls. One story told how he surprised Hercules and his beloved asleep on a moonless night. Unbeknown to Faunus, the two humans had swapped clothes. Faunus whispered sweet nothings in the ear of the sleeping "girl," until the muscular Hercules awoke and sent him packing! After this, to avoid confusion, Faunus insisted his priests wear no clothes. The Romans kept up the tradition in the Lupercalia, a festival celebrated on February 15, when even noble Romans could be found enjoying themselves in the streets naked, save for a goatskin.

WATCHING THE FLOCKS

Only wealthy Romans regularly ate meat, but everybody had ewe's or goat's milk and cheese. Landowners kept flocks of sheep and goats that were

▼ This wall painting from Naples shows Flora stripping blooms as she passes.

▼ In this 19th-century German painting, two fauns watch a sleeping nymph. The Romans believed that a whole race of creatures who were half-man, half-goat lived in the countryside.

GODS OF FRUITFUL HARVESTS

The Romans had many other country gods, some of them very old, others borrowed from the Greeks. Nearly all had to do with the farming year. Ceres taught people to plough, sow, reap, and bake. She was usually shown carrying a sheaf of corn, as a symbol of fruitfulness. She was also pictured searching for her lost daughter Proserpina (see page 16).

Flora was the goddess of springtime, vines, fruit trees, and flowers. Her companion, Pomona, also helped watch over the orchards. Spring festivals to celebrate Flora had a reputation for bawdiness and the blossoming of romances.

guarded mostly by young boys. To pass the time, these young herdsmen played tunes on delicate pipes made from hollowed-out reeds. They used the pipes to help round up the animals for milking.

ECHO AND NARCISSUS

The Roman poet Ovid told this story in his collection of tales Metamorphoses. *It is from an old Greek legend. A handsome youth named Narcissus was so in love with himself that he rejected all the girls who fell for him, including the nymph Echo. The gods were angry and condemned Narcissus to gaze at his own reflection in a pond until he wasted away and died. Only a flower remained, the narcissus. Poor Echo pined for her lost love, and she became just an unseen voice in the rocks and trees. In this painting by Poussin, Narcissus gazes at his reflection while Echo watches from a rock with a love never to be returned.*

BACCHUS AND HIS REVELS

B ACCHUS, another son of Jupiter, was the Roman god of wine. His mother was not a goddess but a human called Semele. The wine god was a handsome young man. Pictures show him riding on a wine barrel, crowned with garlands of vine leaves and grapes, and carrying a goblet. Often he rides in a chariot drawn by leopards. Sometimes he has two horns as a symbol of his power.

▲ Roman wall painting of Bacchus and one of his followers. His coronet is made of vine leaves and flowers.

BACCHUS AND THE PIRATES

Bacchus had many adventures on his travels. Once he was captured by sea pirates, who bound him with thick ropes. But the knots came undone on their own. The sea around the pirate ship turned to wine, and a green vine grew up its mast. Bacchus changed into a roaring lion, and all the pirates, save one, leaped overboard, and were turned into dolphins. One sailor who was spared guided Bacchus to the island of Naxos, where he met his wife-to-be, Ariadne.

◀ This famous painting by Caravaggio shows Bacchus crowned with grapes and vine leaves.

Bacchus had the gift of prophecy, and could assume animal shape. He taught humans to plant grapevines and to make wine, and traveled far to spread the knowledge. For this he became a god himself. He married Ariadne, a Cretan princess.

DRUNKEN REVELS

Bacchus is almost never alone. He is followed first by his friend and tutor Silenus, who was the son of Faunus (see page 26). Then come nymphs, other fauns, shepherds, and female revelers called maenads. These fun-loving followers are always drunkenly singing, dancing, and enjoying themselves.

▲ A pre-Roman vase shows the head of a faun and a maenad, typical followers of the god Bacchus.

▲ In this Roman sculpture, followers of Bacchus bring wine and food to the festivities. Most of his fans were women.

PARTY TIME

Wine played an important part in Roman life, and making it was hard work. Slaves trod the grapes with bare feet, dancing on them rhythmically to the sound of pipes and drums. Once made, the new wine was tasted, and everyone gave thanks to Bacchus. Each year, the Romans held a festival in his honor. It was called the Bacchanalia and was an excuse for drunkenness and wild behavior, which is the meaning of the word "bacchanalian."

GLOSSARY

Aeneas Hero of Roman and Greek stories; his adventures were told in a long poem, the *Aeneid*, by Virgil.

altar Table used for offering up sacrifices.

astrologer Person who studies the supposed effects of the stars on people's lives and actions.

augur Roman who foretold the future by interpreting omens.

bier Frame, like a stretcher, on which a dead person is carried to the grave.

brazier Basket or tray holding hot coals.

bronze Metal alloy made from copper and tin.

bust Sculpture of a person's head, shoulders, and chest.

caduceus Mercury's rod, a wand with two wings on top and two serpents twined around it.

centaur Creature that was half-man, half-horse.

centurion Commander of 100 men in the Roman army.

chariot Wheeled carriage pulled by horses, used in Roman times for racing or in battle.

citadel Fortress in or near a city.

citizen Person living in a city; Roman citizens, but not slaves, had special rights and privileges.

cobbler Shoe-mender.

conch Shell used as a trumpet by the Tritons.

coronet Small crown or headdress.

curse To wish evil on someone.

cypress Cone-bearing tree whose branches were carried at funerals; it eventually became a symbol of death.

distaff Stick that holds a tuft of wool or flax when someone is spinning.

entrails Insides of an animal.

famine Lack of food that affects a large number of people.

faun Creature with a man's head and body, and a goat's horns, hind legs, and tail.

fertility Fruitfulness, producing plenty.

forum Public meeting area or marketplace, especially the Forum in Rome.

garland Necklace or circle of flowers.

genius Spirit of good or evil that accompanied people; plural is genii.

goblet Large drinking cup without a handle.

god Supernatural being who is worshipped.

hearth Place in a house where the fire is lit.

Hercules (Greek Herakles) In Greek myth, hero famous for his strength.

Hippocrates (died about 370 B.C.) Greek physician, known as the father of medicine.

incense Substance burned to give off perfumed smoke, especially during a religious ceremony.

lot Item, such as a long or short straw, drawn in a lottery to decide, for example, who will get a particular task or prize.

lyre Musical instrument like a harp, used to accompany poetry.

maenad Woman who follows the wine-god Bacchus in his revels.

muse One of nine daughters of Jupiter who inspired poetry, music, and other arts.

nereid Sea, or water, nymphs.

nymph Spirit that lives in mountains, seas, rivers, trees, or woodlands; young and beautiful girl-like creature.

omen Sign of a future event, either good or bad.

oratory Art of speaking to an audience, studied in Roman times.

Ovid Roman poet (43 B.C. to A.D. 17?). His poem *Metamorphoses* describes the adventures and love affairs of gods and heroes.

Paris Prince of Troy; he judged a beauty contest between Venus, Juno, and Minerva, and he stole away the Greek princess Helen and so caused the Trojan War.

patrician Person belonging to one of the first families of Rome, an aristocrat of the early Roman Republic.

Pegasus Winged horse, the offspring of Neptune and the Gorgon Medusa.

plebeian Common people of the early Roman Republic: freed slaves, peasants, and farmers.

The map shows the location of Rome and its empire.

ROMAN GOD = GREEK GOD

ROMAN GOD	GREEK GOD
AESCULAPIUS	ASKLEPIOS
APOLLO	APOLLO
BACCHUS	DIONYSOS
CERES	DEMETER
CUPID	EROS
DIANA	ARTEMIS
FAUNUS	PAN
JUNO	HERA
JUPITER	ZEUS
MARS	ARES
MERCURY	HERMES
MINERVA	ATHENA
NEPTUNE	POSEIDON
PLUTO	HADES
SATURN	KRONOS
VENUS	APHRODITE
VESTA	HESTIA
VULCAN	HEPHAISTOS

Pompeii Ancient city in Italy, destroyed and buried in ash by the volcano Vesuvius in A.D. 79.

priest/priestess Person who performs special religious duties.

quiver Pouch in which an archer carries arrows.

religion System of beliefs involving the worship of supernatural powers, identified as gods and goddesses.

ritual Set actions (words, music, offerings) performed as part of religious worship.

sacred Special or holy in a religious sense.

sacrifice Offerings made to a god, such as food and drink, and particularly an animal killed for the purpose.

sheaf Bundle of wheat stalks gathered and bound together at harvest time.

shrine Place with special religious meaning, usually with a small statue of a god or goddess.

soothsayer Person believed to foretell, or divine, the future.

spirit Part of a person that is independent of the body; also a supernatural being, sometimes without a body, but often believed to take human and animal forms.

temple Building set aside for religious worship.

Tiber River in Italy on which Rome stands.

trident Three-pronged fork used to spear fish and used as a weapon by gladiators in the Roman arena.

tutor Teacher; often one hired to teach pupils one-to-one.

underworld Place in which the spirits of the dead dwell.

Vestal Virgin Unmarried woman dedicated to looking after the sacred flame in the temple of the goddess Vesta.

vines Plants on which grapes grow.

Virgil (Publius Vergilius Maro, 70–19 B.C.) Greatest Roman poet; wrote the epic *Aeneid* and poems about country life.

INDEX

Page numbers in *italics* refer to illustrations.